Jill and the Beanstalk

Written by Gill and Paul Hamlyn

Illustrated by Kevin McAleenan

Rigby

There was a giant
who lived in the sky.
He took Jill's things –
Oh, my! Oh, my!

Jill climbed the beanstalk,
and she didn't stop.
She climbed and climbed
till she reached the top.

Jill saw the giant
fast asleep.

Jill came in,
creep, creep, creep.

She took her harp.

She took her hen.

She took her bag
of money ... then

5

the giant shouted,
"No, no, no!"

Jill knew then
it was time to go.

Jill took an axe
and began to chop.
The giant bellowed
"Stop, stop, stop!"

The giant fell down
on his head.
Jill had her things
and the giant was dead.